OMFG,

BEES!

OMFG,
BEES!

Bees Are So Amazing and You're About to Find Out Why

Matt Kracht

CHRONICLE BOOKS

SAN FRANCISCO

Library of Congress Cataloging-in-Publication Data available.

ISBN 978-1-7972-1990-5

Manufactured in China.

MIX
Paper | Supporting
responsible forestry
FSC™ C008047

Design by Maggie Edelman.

10 9 8 7 6 5 4 3 2 1

Chronicle books and gifts are available at special quantity
discounts to corporations, professional associations, literacy
programs, and other organizations. For details and discount
information, please contact our premiums department at
corporatesales@chroniclebooks.com or at 1-800-759-0190.

Chronicle Books LLC
680 Second Street
San Francisco, California 94107

www.chroniclebooks.com

CONTENTS

Introduction

As I sit down to write this introduction, it is a warm spring day, and you know what that means. That's right, it means BEES!!!!

If you do not yet fully grasp why this is so goddamned exciting, just relax, because I am going to tell you all about it in this amazing book, and when I'm done, you will want to thank me for helping you see how incredible bees are.

Now, I realize that some people don't like bees, but we will ignore them because bees are definitely where it's at, Jack.

Plus, did you know that without bees we all die of an apple deficiency? It's called ecology. Seriously, bees are so important to our agricultural food supply that we should be kissing bees' asses.

Actually, don't literally do this because, while they do deserve our deepest gratitude, they do not like to be kissed by us and you should respect that.

In closing, long introductions are boring, so let's get on with the BEES!!!!

Matt Kracht
Tacoma, Washington
Spring 2023

A NOTE TO ASPIRING COPY EDITORS REGARDING THE SPELLING OF COMMON BEE NAMES IN THIS BOOK

If you are an entomologist, a science-journal proofreader, or just some sort of weird pedant, then this section is for you. The rest of you are free to move on if you prefer.

Most of us are used to seeing the word "honeybee." An entomologist will tell you that "honey bee" is the accepted spelling according to the Entomological Society of America (ESA), whose naming rules require that a name be broken into separate words whenever the common name accurately describes the scientific order to which the insect belongs. But unless you are an entomologist and can recall the order of every bug you've ever seen, you're never going to know whether it's ladybug or lady bug. (Either way, "FU," says the ESA Common Names database, "it's actually lady beetle.")

I am a big fan of science so, out of respect for the real experts, whose diligent pursuit of scientific knowledge about bees has made my research for this book possible, I will attempt to faithfully adhere to the ESA's rules when referring to the common names of insects.

Except for "honeybee" and "bumblebee"—it just looks stupid to break them apart and I won't do it.

People Who Don't Like Bees

I know I said we were going to ignore them, but in hindsight, that seems unfair. I myself have some mixed feelings about nature—while I do mostly enjoy it, if I'm honest, there are parts that I really like and some that I don't really care for.

I'm sure you know what I mean. For instance, many people enjoy getting outdoors for a nice summer hike, but they hate ticks and mosquitoes. Some people like a good swim but are creeped out by the feel of kelp in their toes. Some people don't like spiders (I mean, I get it, who needs eight legs?). Like many people, I despise birds. Some people hate rocks or pine cones, but those people should be avoided. A lot of nature is made out of dirt, but most of us own a vacuum cleaner or a broom. Where was I?

Oh, right. Some people don't like bees, and what the hell is up with that??

Yes, it would be easy to judge people who don't like bees. They must be assholes, right? In some cases, yes, but that may not have anything to do with how they feel about bees.

My theory is that most individuals who say they don't like bees are actually decent people who just had a very bad experience with a bee, and/or they are allergic, so therefore their fear of pain and death is heightened when bees are nearby.

Mathematically speaking, bee trauma plus your bee allergy coefficient divided by distance in meters to the nearest bee equals how you feel about bees. Not everyone is great at mathematics, so I have devised a visual matrix to illustrate this principle. I call this the *Fear-Based Bee Opinion Matrix*, or the F-BOM.

Childhood traumas aside, there is no real need to fear bees, unless you are some kind of maniac who goes around smacking bees' nests with a stick or swatting at them whenever they come close to you— then you probably should be afraid, because those bees might decide to mess you up, and who could blame them?

Anyway, with few exceptions, bees are fairly docile if they are not antagonized. Ordinarily, they will only sting if they feel that you are messing with them, so if you do get stung there's a pretty good chance that you had it coming.

F-BOM Matrix

a↑y   trauma

BEE! BEE!!
X omg omg omg
get it OFF!
Ahhhh!

‐ Have HAD TO USE EpiPEN
MULTIPLE TIMES due to BEES

X I hate
bees!

‐ STUNG AS young CHILD
X I don't like
bees, ok?

X get away
from me, bee!

X oh shit, a bee!

Neutral
about
bees

──────────────→ m   distance

0.0 m   ∞

X BEES
ARE ALRIGHT.

X Oh, hello, bee!
I won't hurt
you ☺

X Bees Are
So cool!

X Let me   (sigh)
tell you   X one day
about bees.   my bees
               will return to me.

X psspsspss
(whispering secrets
to bee.)

‐ BEE SPOKE TO YOU AS CHILD,
PROMISED YOU WOULD ONE DAY
BE GRANTED ABILITY TO
FLY WITH BEES...

(negative trauma)

a = severity of allergy
y = bee trauma
m = proximity to nearest bee in meters

$$\frac{a+y}{m} =$$

(no allergy = 0)

Not everyone
can be good
with numbees,
ok?

BEES AND NOT-BEES

Before we go any further let's get a few things straight:
When it comes to striped, flying insects that might sting
you, there are bees, and then there are not-bees (I know
we're all anxious to get on with the bees, but that is what the
rest of this book is about, so I'm going to skip them for now.
Don't worry about it, we'll get to the bees soon enough).

Not-bees include:

HOVER FLIES
WASPS
HORNETS

Hover fly

Sad.

two wings

Always hovering around

Eupeodes americanus

Wasps

These vicious little turds can sometimes be mistaken for bees, especially if you are eight years old and running for your very life from an angry swarm of them because you had the idea to conduct a major scientific experiment wherein you bang a stick on the metal clothesline pole in your grandpa's backyard in order to determine what kind of sound it makes.

In the course of this experiment you would have discovered that the soft, metallic ringing is pleasant to your human ears, but apparently enraging to wasps, and also that open-ended metal pipes used to make clothesline poles sometimes house wasps' nests.

As a junior scientist, you would have noted an unexpected result of the pole-banging to be a group of about a half dozen small striped insects shooting from the pole at high speed in a tight V formation, like a squadron of tiny RAF Spitfires diving out of the sky at a lost enemy bomber over the English Channel!

Anyway, wasps are categorically not bees. They are insects related to bees and ants, and while many are pollinators and predators of other insects (making them valuable to agriculture), they are mean goddamn sons of bitches with no sense of fair play.

Here are some different wasp bastards that you are likely to encounter.

YELLOWJACKETS

Vespula vulgaris, or yellowjackets (they just call them "wasps" in Europe). These bastards are the most common type of wasp, and the most aggressive. They are attracted to the sugars in fallen and rotting fruit, which is a food source, but they also like meat and will openly fight with you over that last bite of hot dog on your plate at the company picnic. I suggest you just slide that plate as far from you as you can without any sudden movements and let them take what they want. It's kind of like being mugged.

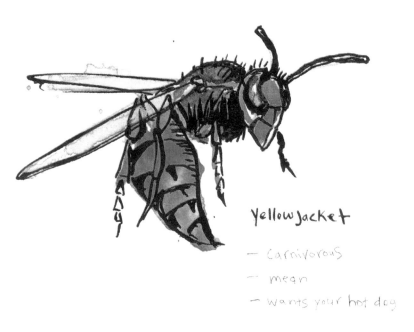

yellowjacket

— carnivorous

— mean

— wants your hot dog

PAPER WASPS

These wasps are part of the *Polistinae* subfamily of the family *Vespidae.* They are named for the paperlike, open-celled nests that they build out of saliva and plant fibers gathered from stems and dead wood. They are pollinators and feed on other insects, such as caterpillars and beetle larvae, so they are very important to the environment in terms of biocontrol and are considered beneficial by many gardeners. Unlike the very aggressive yellowjacket, paper wasps will typically only attack in response to a threat to their nest, e.g., a junior scientist banging a stick on the metal tube that houses them.

Paper Wasp

Waspy.

Polistes fuscatus

MUD DAUBERS

These are the ones that are always making those little mud huts on your porch or in your yard. They are sometimes called "mud wasps" and they belong to either the family *Crabronidae* or *Sphecidae*, but not *Vespidae* (those guys are damned potter wasps). They are solitary, so they don't create hives, but instead build a clay-based compartment to house their eggs and larvae, to which they feed paralyzed caterpillars and spiders. They're not super aggressive toward people unless you disturb them. My advice? Leave them alone and they will usually leave you alone, sort of like cats, except that cats will ignore you all the time, so I guess this is not a very good comparison. The two main things to remember here are try to avoid disturbing mud daubers, and cats can be very selfish.

Mud dauber

Wad of
Mud

Sceliphron caementarium
(AKA the " black and yellow mud dauber")

Hornets

All hornets belong to the genus *Vespa* and are technically eusocial* wasps. In fact, they are the largest of the wasps. There are just over twenty species of hornet recognized in the world, and most are native to Asia. But the European hornet (*Vespa crabro*) is native to Europe. It is the only true hornet found in North America, having been brought over by some apparently dumbass European settlers in the 1800s. They are carnivorous and feed on other insects, but also enjoy sugary fruits. They are not overly aggressive, usually only stinging when stepped on or touched, or if you get around their nest or too near a food source. So basically they might sting you at any moment for any reason, but other than that, they're pretty chill.

European hornet

enjoys fruit, plus also killing and eating other insects

Vespa crabro

* Eusocial species are those that live in a multigenerational colony in which the majority of individuals work to provide food, protection, and care of the young for a small reproductive group, usually one female and multiple males.

Many bees, like honeybees, are eusocial—but bees are not the only animals who are. For instance, there are eusocial ants and termites. Naked mole rats are eusocial, and also creepy as hell.

A Note on Murder Hornets

Its real name is the northern giant hornet (formerly the Asian giant hornet), and it is the largest known hornet in the world.

God help us if they ever discover a hornet bigger than *Vespa mandarinia*, because just thinking about being caught in a room with one of these monstrous shitheads will give you a case of the sweating terrors.

This flying nightmare measures almost 2 inches [5 cm] in length and has a 3 inch [7.5 cm] wingspan. As if its body size were not intimidating enough, its stinger is a solid ¼ inch [6 mm], which is four times longer than a honeybee's, and it can puncture a beekeeper's jacket.

"Haha," you say, "no, thank you! That's more than enough terror for me!" Well, too bad. Grab a fresh pair of pants, because there's more.

It carries an extremely potent venom—those stung have described feeling like a red-hot nail is being driven through their flesh. While it does not technically have the most potent wasp venom in the world, this sadistic son of a bitch makes up for that by injecting an extra-large dose into its victims, making multiple stings potentially deadly to humans, even those who are not allergic.

They are considered "extremely predatory," hunting other wasps and hornets, and even killing the occasional rodent when the mood strikes them, the sick bastards.

Oh, and did I mention that they are also known for spraying venom into the eyes? Jesus.

But aside from all that, what they seem to really delight in is murdering honeybees.

- Huge
- Kills bees
- scary as hell

for murder

5cm!
(that's like 2 inches)

DANGER!

Vespa mandarinia

northern giant hornet

When one of these hornets finds a beehive, they will kill individual bees and bring the bodies home as a food source. This will go on for a while, but eventually, the hornet will come back with a team of about thirty friends and just start grabbing bees and nonchalantly decapitating them, ripping their heads off one by one, until they've wiped out all the bees in the colony. It is a few hours of merciless bloody chaos and mayhem, and the honeybees have no chance.

The wholesale slaughter phase is followed by the hive occupation phase, where the hornets make themselves at home among the thousands of headless bee bodies in the hive for a few days while they kill all the defenseless bee larvae, which they remove and use to feed their own brood of evil young.

The whole thing is like a 1970s horror movie, only worse because it's real! (But also better because, let's be honest, most of those movies were crap.)

Once found only in parts of Asia, these stone-cold bee terminators have been discovered in recent years in Vancouver, British Columbia, and Washington State.

While nests are currently believed to be limited to a small area of the Pacific Northwest, it is feared that if they become established in North America, they could quickly decimate the population of honeybees and become so entrenched that they could never be eradicated. This would be bad news for honeybees, not to mention everyone who likes to eat food grown by farmers.

If you spot one of these murdering bastards, contact the local authorities, for Christ's sake.

No seriously, you actually need to call your state apiary inspector. It is recommended that you exercise "appropriate precautions," whatever the hell that means, and, if you can do so safely, take a picture and report it ASAP (in the US: https://apiaryinspectors.org/us-inspection-services).

STANDARD Bee Parts

There's some other parts, but
lets not get ahead of ourselves, ok?

Head

Antennae
(1 or 2)

the eye
(compound)
eyes

also an eye

wings
(duh) *

forewing

Legs

hindwing

tarsal claws

pollen basket!!

"thorax"
It's true,
look it up!

Abdomen
(the tummy)

STINGER!!
one-time use!

What Is a Bee?

Now that we've talked about what aren't bees, we can get down to actual important things, like "What IS a bee?"

A scientist would probably tell you that bees are flying insects that collect pollen and nectar. They are known for their pollination of plants and, in some cases, for producing honey. There are possibly as many as 20,000 individual species of bees, and they are considered a clade called *Anthophila*, which belongs to the superfamily *Apoidea* of the order *Hymenoptera*.

A bee would probably say, "Hey, what's your problem, science guy? How come you so-called 'scientists' are always trying to act like you get to label us? You don't know me!"

Then I would say, "Shhh . . . don't worry about that dude, bee. He's just trying to order the world by classifying everything. By doing the labeling, he places himself symbolically above other species . . . I guess it makes him feel smart. These scientists have deep-seated insecurities."

And the bee would be like, "Whatever, I don't have time for this clown. Come on, let's bounce and go find a good flower."

* Bees actually have four wings! So what? Each pair of front and back wings hooks together when they fly — that's what! (This creates more LIFT, which is both efficient and badass.)

THE SEVEN FAMILIES OF BEES

When I say "The Seven Families of Bees," you might think, "The Seven Families of Bees?!? What the hell is that? Is that the title of a bestselling coming-of-age novel? Is it a new docudrama miniseries? Or maybe a kick-ass martial arts movie about Bee-Style Kung Fu?"

Wow, I have to admit, that would be a super cool movie—I like the way you think!

But actually, no. What I am talking about here is that there are seven families of bees in terms of biological classification. You know, *Kingdom, Phylum, Class, Order, Family* . . . the science-y families.

Phylogenetic Classification of Bees

Kingdom ———→ Animalia
Phylum ———→ Arthropoda
Class ———→ Insecta
Order ———→ Hymenoptera
family →⎰ Andrenidae
⎱ Apidae
Colletidae
Halictidae
Megachilidae
Melittidae
Stenotritidae

this is literally what we are talking about

All the bees

Andrenidae

You've probably heard of these little guys. They're smaller than honeybees and most of them are black with white or light tan hair. They're commonly known as "mining bees" because they nest in the ground. They are solitary, which means no hive for these bees. In early spring both males and females emerge from their nests and then they mate, after which the female is like, "So long, Charlie, it's been great," and goes off to find a site for her nest burrow. She builds little cells, each holding a little ball made of pollen and nectar, plus an egg. She seals them up for the winter, but check this out: They will emerge as BEES next spring! There are a lot of different species of bees in this family, and they're all free spirits.

Mining bees

Calliopsis rhodophila

Apidae

This bee family is definitely where it's at because it includes the most classic bees: bumblebees and honeybees, baby!!!!! It also has some other real interesting characters, like long-horned bees, *Diadasia* bees, *Anthrophora* bees, carpenter bees, and those crazy-ass orchid bees. That's a shitload of different bees, so there's something for everyone.

look at that crazy long tongue

(great for getting into those orchids)

Green Orchid bee

Euglossa dilemma

Colletidae

These babies are often called "plasterer bees" because they coat the lining of their nests with a secretion from their mouths that dries into a waterproof coating like cellophane. Holy crap, did you just read that?? Also, they're nocturnal. Well, technically they're *crepuscular*, meaning primarily active during the twilight hours, but still. Night-bees!!!

plasterer bees are sometimes called "polyester bees"

they never wear polyester.

Caupolicana electa

Halictidae

These are called "sweat bees," which sounds gross, I know. But hold on! They're not gross or sweaty, they're attracted to sweat. I mean, yeah, that does sound a little gross, I guess. But it's just because they need salt! Bees: They're just like us.

Sweat bees live all over the world, so you may have seen one. Many have brightly colored metallic green, blue, or red bodies, which is, I don't know . . . INCREDIBLE. If you think about it, that's way cooler than the standard human, who only comes in a boring dull matte finish. This is why we invented gold lamé jumpsuits.

"green sweat bee"

shiny!

this bee rocks

Augochloropsis metallica

Megachilidae

These crazy mothers carry pollen exclusively on the under-side of their abdomens and don't even bother with carrying it on their hind legs like most other bees—don't tell *them* how to carry their pollen! The *Megachilidae* family includes mason bees, leafcutter bees, resin bees, and carder bees, each named for the material they use in making their nests (soil, leaves, plant resins, or animal fibers).

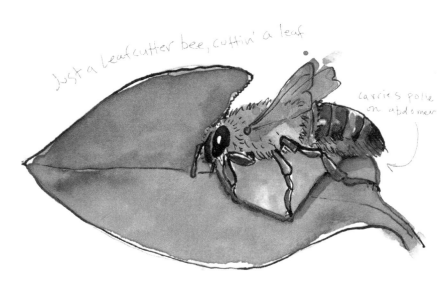

Just a leafcutter bee, cuttin' a leaf

carries pollen on abdomen

Megachile centuncularis

Melittidae

This is a small family of bees, with just over two hundred species. They are solitary and live primarily in drier climates in Africa and the northern temperate zone, where they dig nesting burrows in the ground. Other bees typically visit many different plants for pollen or nectar, but the *Melittidae* are oligolectic pollinators. This means that they are total specialists in certain types of flowers and often feed exclusively on a single genus or family of plants—basically, they are very picky about what they pollinate, unlike a certain cousin of mine who will remain unnamed, but for god's sake, have some self-respect, Jeff.

oligolectic

very
particular
about where
they dine.

Macropis europaea

Stenotritidae

Damn, there are only twenty-one species of *Stenotritidae*, and they all live in Australia! How the hell did Australia get so lucky? These bees burrow and are big, fast, and really hairy, which, if you think about it, sounds a lot like a dog. Wait. Oh my god, what if you could cross a dog with a bee? How cool would that be? I would name him Buzz. Anyway, Stenotritidae were formerly considered part of the *Colletidae* family, but they got promoted to being their own family in 1980, thanks to cool bee-scientist Ronald J. McGinley.

Big

fast!

Hairy

Lovable

Ctenocolletes nigricans
(Stenotritidae)

A NOTE ON CUCKOO BEES

"Cuckoo bee" is really sort of a catchall term for different bees of various families that have all evolved to lay their eggs in the nests of other bees (kind of like how the cuckoo bird lays her eggs in another bird's nest and lets that chump feed and raise her young, but don't even get me started on birds). This is called kleptoparasitism, and it's sort of cheating, but it's also pretty smart if you ask me. Female cuckoo bees don't have any apparatus for carrying pollen, and they don't build their own nests. Why? Because they don't need to, do they???

BEE JOBS

Believe it or not, life as a bee isn't all just flying around, pollinating flowers, and looking fantastic. There's a lot of important work to be done, so every bee has to do their part.

Social Bees

Social bees live in various types of communities, but when there are overlapping generations with cooperative brood care and a division of labor into reproductive and non-reproductive castes, we call it "eusociality"—for example, honeybees, stingless bees, and some types of bumblebees are eusocial.

I know this might sound complicated, but relax. Basically it just means that each bee in the hive has one of three very specific job descriptions, and they have it for life.

WORKER

They constitute the vast majority of the bees in the colony. While these infertile females are the smallest of the three castes, they're called "workers" because these are the bees that get shit done around here. They build the nest. They collect the pollen and nectar. They make the honey. They ventilate the hive with their wings to regulate the temperature and keep it from getting too humid. They keep the larvae fed, they tend to the drones, they tend to the queen, and if the queen stops laying eggs, they replace that bitch by making a new one. These bees are the real deal.

DRONE

The male bees are called "drones" and are generally larger than the female worker bees.

"Hold it," you're probably thinking. "You just said that the females do all the stuff! So just what exactly is it that the males do?"

That's an excellent question, and thanks for asking. The technical answer is "a whole lot of nothing, apparently," because the drones do no goddamn work around the hive at all. Turns out they're just there to mate with the queen. Typical.

Other than reproducing, they mostly just take up space lounging around all day, I guess. Hell, they don't even have stingers. Honestly, they are next to useless as a bee.

Often right before winter when food sources get scarce, the females will kick their lazy male asses right out of the hive. Beat it, losers, and don't bother with that "Baby, please!" bullshit, either.

SORRY TO DRONE ON

We know drones don't do much work around the hive. They may not have stingers, but they *do* have larger compound eyes than the other bee castes. This is not just to make them look extra hunky; it also helps them see better, which is important when they follow the queen out of the hive and up into the air for her mating flight. Seriously, it's really all they're good for.

Honeybee Jobs

Worker

drone

Queen

QUEEN

The queen is by far the largest of the three castes, and if you're going to be a bee, this is probably the job you'd want. Unfortunately, there's only ever one queen per hive, so your odds aren't great.

You'd think she must have it pretty good, just ordering everybody around and being groomed and fed by workers all day, but actually she's not as much in charge as you'd imagine, given her title. Her whole job is to reproduce and, while that means she doesn't have to gather pollen or do any of that other standard bee drudgery, she will lay between 1,000 and 6,000 eggs every single day, which keeps her pretty busy.

When a colony gets big enough, the queen may decide to move on and fly away, taking a portion of the other bees with her to find a place to form a new colony. This is called "swarming."

The remaining workers in the original colony are like, "Oh, well, that's just perfect. I guess we'll just produce a whole new batch of potential queens because we didn't have enough to do around here already." They do this by feeding a high-nutrient food called "royal jelly" to a number of female larvae, which will then develop into virgin queens in their specially constructed queen chambers.

Once a virgin queen hatches, she looks for any other potential virgin queen rivals in the hive and kills them, unless they kill her first. This is a pretty bitchy thing to do to your sisters, but that's just the way it is because there can be only one bee on the throne. Just look at all of European history if you don't believe me.

Anyway, once all of the competition has been eliminated, the victorious virgin queen goes out on the town to celebrate and mate with a whole boatload of drones, maybe a dozen or more, if possible. After mating, the males just drop dead, because that's all they're good for, and the now-not-so-virgin queen returns to the hive and lays eggs for the rest of her two-to-seven-year life. Nice work if you can get it.

Solitary Bees

While the eusocial bees have their lifelong work castes within the colony, some other bees do not live this way. Many bees, such as mason bees, carpenter bees, and leaf-cutter bees, are called "solitary bees," meaning they do not live communally.

In solitary bee species, each female is fertile and makes her own nest, laying many eggs. When the eggs hatch, each of the females is also fertile and will go on to mate and lay her own brood. So there are no reproductive caste distinctions, no queen, and no worker. The males are still just there for the mating, of course.

Some people with traditional views about bees' roles might be shocked to hear all of this, but that's because they are uptight. I think you really have to admire their courage. These bees don't give a crap about the societal expectations of a eusocial hive, or anybody else's ideas about bee gender roles, either—they're out there every day, doing it *their* way, trying to live their authentic best life on their own damned terms, and I think that's great. I stand in solidarity with the solitary bee.

HOW DO BEES MAKE HONEY?

No one knows exactly how bees make honey but, haha, I am messing with you, we totally know how bees make honey, and I am here to tell you all about it.

But before we dive into how they make it, let's start with what honey *is*. You probably think you know everything you need to know about honey, but let me break it down anyway. Trust me, this is good stuff.

Honey has been a prized sweetener and valuable commodity to humankind for thousands of years. In fact, there is archaeological evidence, including *cave paintings* of bees and honey collecting, that prehistoric farmers were already gathering honey as far back as 9,000 years ago!

(As a sidenote, bears and badgers have been gathering honey since before anyone can remember, so we were hardly the first to the honey party, but we were the first to document it. As far as we're aware, anyway . . . I mean, bears suck at painting, so we might never know whether they beat us to it, because it would probably just be some messy yellow smudges on a tree and nothing you could recognize as bees. Haha, nice try, bears.)

Anyway, honey is sweet and delicious, and it makes peanut butter toast worth eating. It is composed primarily of sugars, but also contains amino acids, vitamins, minerals like iron and zinc, and antioxidants. It has anti-inflammatory properties, works as a cough suppressant, and has been linked in studies to a number of potential health benefits, including reduced risk of heart disease, faster wound healing, and memory loss prevention, among other things.

Holy crap, that's some pretty incredible stuff! But I almost forgot to mention the most unbelievable thing about honey, which is that *bees* make it. Bees!

Worker bees begin leaving the hive when they are about three weeks old to forage for pollen and nectar. (This seems pretty young to have to work outside the home, but they only live about two months, so it's really more like middle age.) Each of these foragers ventures out in search of flowers and can carry her own body weight in nectar, which is impressive, especially if you've ever tried to carry your own body weight in anything while flying.

Unlike moths, which drink nectar by sucking it through their nasty mothy proboscis (gross), bees on a nectar-gathering mission drink by dipping their little bee tongues rapidly in and out of the nectar. This is adorable, and it is also very precise and efficient, which is 100 percent on-brand for a honeybee.

HIVE A NICE DAY

Although the terms are used interchangeably these days, a "beehive" is technically a man-made structure used to house a colony of domesticated honeybees, whereas a "nest" is naturally occurring and may be home to any number of bee species, honey producing or not.

While they lack the architectural charm of more traditional beehives, modern-day box hives are well-designed structures involving tops that open and a removable comb-frame design that allows for easy collection of honey without much damage or trauma to the colony.

The distinctive dome shape that we now associate with beehives (and often see used to symbolize bees, honey, or industry) comes from an ancient beehive design called a *skep,* which was an upside-down basket woven from wicker and then coated in mud and dung. Skeps and their open-interior design meant that harvesting honey was difficult and often required killing all of the bees first. The beekeeper had to upend the skep and cut out the entire honeycomb. In some cases, the honey was extracted by putting the skep in a vise, which seems overly dramatic and, I can only imagine, would lead to what most modern consumers would consider an unacceptable dung-to-honey ratio.

Box Beehive

Skep Beehive

The bee stores this nectar in a special stomach called the "honey stomach" or "nectar sac." If she gets tired, she can open a special valve in the sac to release some of the sugar-rich nectar into her regular bee stomach to be converted into energy. Go ahead, read that again. It's basically *mid-flight self-refueling.* INSANE! But the honeybees are like, "No big deal, I was born for this."

When she returns to her home base, she delivers her sugary payload to an indoor bee. Then that nectar is passed, by mouth, from bee to bee in the hive, which introduces a special bee enzyme from their saliva (it's called "invertase," and it breaks down the sucrose in the nectar). Then it is put into the open hexagonal cells of the honeycomb and left until the moisture content has been reduced down from about 70 percent to 20 percent and the nectar turns into honey.

Okay, I just need a minute, because holy shit that is INCREDIBLE. Call it chemistry and evaporation, but wow. Is there anything bees can't do? I mean, yes, obviously. But still, just wow.

Anyway, after that, workers use wax to seal the honey in for storage. It will be mixed later with pollen to make "bee bread," which is high in sugars and protein, and will be fed to the young when the eggs hatch. The honey reserves will help the colony survive through the winter when food is scarce. (That, and kicking the males out of the hive).

BOOM. Honey.

How do bees make honey

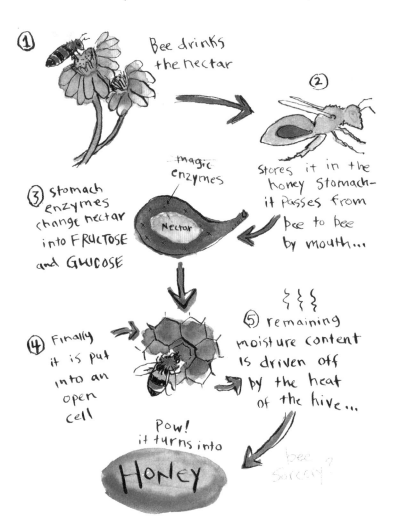

① Bee drinks the nectar

② Stores it in the honey Stomach - it passes from bee to bee by mouth...

magic enzymes

③ stomach enzymes change nectar into FRUCTOSE and GLUCOSE

Nectar

④ Finally it is put into an open cell

⑤ remaining moisture content is driven off by the heat of the hive...

Pow! it turns into

HONEY

bee sorcery?

Oh My God,
It's Not All about Honey

All right, we all agree that honey is amazing. But not all bees make honey. In fact, out of roughly twenty thousand species of bees, maybe a hundred of them make honey, and they're all in the family *Apidae*. Yeah, that's right, most bee species don't make any honey at all.

And so what? Does a bee need to be an endless source of your honey for them to be valued and appreciated? Bees aren't just here to pump out the sweet stuff so you can drizzle it all over your plain organic yogurt without a second thought. They don't get up and go to work every single day just so you can pour their hard-earned honey into your chamomile-and-nettle tea in an attempt to make it vaguely palatable. As if you even like that tea.

Most bees are just trying to live their lives and feed their larvae like anyone else. And let me remind you that, meanwhile, they're also pollinating our gardens and our crops without so much as a "thank you," and if you could get your drooling and slavering for sweet, delicious honey under control for one minute, you might think about showing a little gratitude for that, too. Jesus, what are you, a hungry bear?

Let's Talk about Hex

We've all heard of honeycomb, but what is it exactly?

Honeycomb is critical to bees of the *Apis* family and is made of beeswax. It is a mass of interlocking hexagonal cells built by honeybees to store pollen, nectar, and honey, and to house the brood.

Honeycomb is something that only honey-producing bees make. Why this is the case should not be a great big mystery. If some of you don't know, stop and think about it for a moment. If you are still struggling with it after a couple of minutes, that's okay, forget about it and just enjoy the pictures in the book from here on out.

The honeycomb is one of the most studied cellular structures in the natural world because of its distinctive hexagonal construction. One could get extremely mathy about it, if one were inclined to show off their math prowess and were also unaware that no one besides another mathematician is ever entertained by that shit. But let's cut to the chase and just say that what *is* so fascinating about honeycomb is that it is built by bees and, while they could make it any shape they want, it is invariably constructed of interlocking hexagons.

Making wax cells to house the brood and store food consumes time, energy, and resources, so if you are a bee you'd want to avoid any wasted space. Obviously. But why not interlocking squares, or even triangles, instead of the complicated six-sided polygon with all those 120-degree angles? People have been wondering about it since probably before geometry was invented.

Enter Marcus Terentius Varro. He was considered one of ancient Rome's greatest scholars, and you know how that can really inflate an ancient nerd's ego. In 36 BCE, Varro conjectured that using the hexagon would create the most compact and thus the most efficient honeycomb structure. This idea has been the prevailing belief among scholars since then and is now called the "Honeycomb Conjecture." (I'm going to let you in on a little secret here: "Conjecture" is what scholars call it when they think they are right but are really just guessing.)

Anyway, it turns out he was a good guesser because in 1999, only a little over two thousand years later, a University of Michigan mathematician named Thomas Hales put an end to the conjecture and proved that a regular hexagonal grid or honeycomb is the best way to divide a surface into regions of equal area with the least total perimeter, and he proved that shit by using math.

So, hexagons make the most sense in terms of wax efficiency, and we know that honeybees love some good efficiency. But how the hell do they do it? Bees can do a lot of amazing things, but as far as we know, using a protractor is not one of them.

But they don't even need to know geometry because it all starts with the bee. Workers begin by chewing bits of wax until it becomes moldable, and then use their legs, mandibles, and even antennae to form a circular cell. This cell will be the circumference of their own thorax, and because all of the workers in the colony are the same size, the cells will be uniform. The next cell is built adjacent to that, and so on. Honeybees maintain the temperature of the nest at 30 to 35 degrees Celsius [86 to 95 degrees Fahrenheit], which just so happens to be the temperature at which beeswax is most malleable but not liquid.

Because all of these circular tubes are built next to each other, the heat from all of those hot worker bees transforms the circular tubes into their iconic rounded hexagon shape via a process involving the flow of molten viscoelastic wax near the triple junction of adjacent cells.

However you look at it, it still seems like some kind of powerful bee magic to me. Can you construct a perfect wax hexagon the exact size of your body without using tools of any kind?? You absolutely cannot.

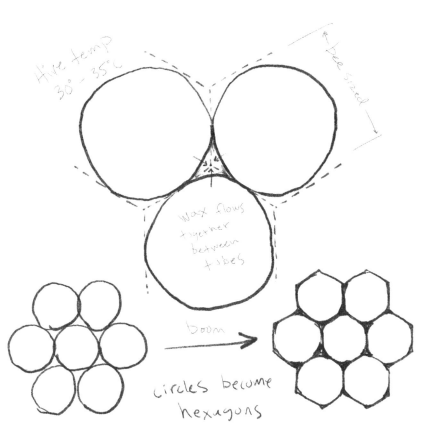

Hive temp
30° - 35°C

bee sized

Wax flows
together
between
tubes

boom →

circles become
hexagons

BEES ARE SMARTER THAN YOU THINK

One might assume that bees aren't very smart. After all, they're insects with brains less than 2 cubic millimeters (that's *0.0002 percent* the size of a human brain) that house less than a million neurons. Dumb as rocks, right?

Wrong, and also FU, because bees manage a lot of impressive behavior and learning in spite of their relatively small brains. They are able to sense and interpret pheromones, odors, tastes, and colors (even ultraviolet); they form cognitive maps of their environment; and they communicate complex information in order to coordinate with one another.

Because of this, bees are one of scientists' favorite animals to model in the study of intelligence, perception, and cognition. I suppose you could also study dolphins, but as any marine biologist can tell you, their laugh is annoying and their breath smells like fish.

Bee Learning

We know that honeybees are very good at associative learning* and this allows them to be efficient foragers who focus their efforts on flowers that offer the best reward, even modifying their foraging patterns over time as conditions change.

"Sure, sure, they're real good at doing bee things," you say. "Big whoop."

But check this out: It seems that they are also good problem solvers, and they can learn to accomplish tasks that have nothing to do with natural bee behavior—even *ones that involve using a new tool*. In one study, bumblebees learned to roll a ball into a hole in order to trigger access to sucrose. They learned how by watching a researcher prod the ball into the hole using a fake bee on a stick. What's more, it was a pretty bad fake bee that I doubt fooled anyone, but the bumblebees were too polite to say anything and just watched the technique. They were able to repeat it after one viewing and then even figured out how to do it more efficiently over successive attempts, which I would find pretty embarrassing if I were that researcher with the dubious-looking bee puppet on a stick.

Scientists once believed that only humans used tools, and that this was evidence that we are the only intelligent species on the block. However, over time, we discovered that a variety of primates, marine animals, and birds use tools. And now we've seen that bees can learn to manipulate human-made objects to complete a task, leading us to the discovery that those scientists were arrogant dipshits.

Dance Language

This sounds like the name of a summer-term elective course, co-taught by the Anthropology Department chair and that weird professor from the School of the Arts, but that's not what we are talking about here. What we *are* here to talk about is the bee dance language, and more specifically the honeybee "waggle-dance," and it's pretty goddamned unbelievable.

First of all, when it comes to dancing, honeybees can really get down. But it's way more than just sweet moves and a great sense of rhythm. For the bees, dancing is a form of communication, and I don't mean that like in some artistic, Martha-Graham-interpretive-dance sort of way, I mean like literally the communication of specific objective information.

When forager bees return to the hive after locating a really choice patch of nectary, pollen-loaded flowers, they naturally want to tell their sisters all about it so that everybody can get in on the action. The other foragers are like, "Hell, yeah, we all-in for the poll-in," but she still needs to give them directions to get there, which is a challenge because the city obviously doesn't assign street addresses to miscellaneous patches of clover.

So she tells them where to go by doing the waggle-dance—it's a way that successful foragers can communicate the location of the food source to the others. The dancer runs in a straight line on an interior wall of the hive, waggling her abdomen and emitting a low-frequency buzzing sound made by beating her wings. She then returns to her starting point via a semicircle, waggles through the straight line again, then returns via another semicircle in the opposite direction, creating a figure eight to complete her moves.

Now get this, and I swear I am not making it up: The dancer aligns her body at an angle indicating the direction from the hive to the food source, *relative to the sun on the horizon.* For example, straight up means directly in line with the sun from the hive, so 15 degrees to the right of that means 15 degrees to the right of the sun on the horizon.

The intensity of her waggle indicates the quality of the food source, and the length of it communicates the distance from the hive to its location (in "bee talk," one second of waggle translates to about half a mile [around 1,000 m].

She also releases a number of pheromones into the air while she does the dance, probably to send out the signal, "Check my moves, bitches! I got the location of some fine flowers just waitin' to be foraged over here!"

There is even evidence that the honeybees who don't fly out to that spot right away are able to adjust for the movement of the sun over time, and thus are still able to successfully calculate the location of the flowers later.

Holy shit, that's some next-level navigation.

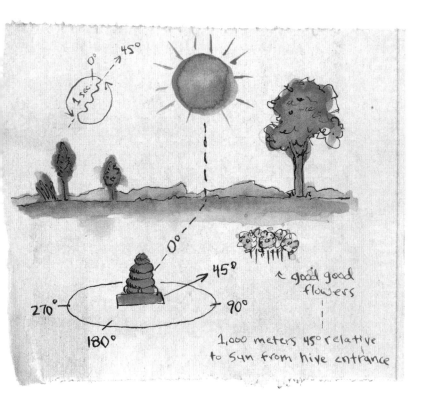

You're Pollen My Leg

It looks like colorful powder, but pollen is really the microspores of a seed plant and, if you're a bee, it's gonna get stuck all over your fuzzy little body. There's no avoiding it. As a bee travels from flower to flower, pollen gets carried from the male structures of one plant to the female structures of another, where plant fertilization occurs, and boom! That's pollination.

A bee might visit between 50 and 1,000 plants per day to gather pollen, depending on how much pollen those plants have available. An average colony of honeybees needs to collect about 100 pounds [45.4 kg] of pollen per season because it is a critical part of a bee's diet. Pollen provides a key source of protein, carbohydrates, vitamins, and minerals, as well as other nutrients. This is why they're always messing around in those flowers.

But how exactly do they collect that pollen and transport it back to the colony? You might be thinking, "Oh, I know the answer to this one," but don't get cocky, because you probably don't know the whole story and the other half is going to blow your mind.

As a bee flies through the air, the extreme rapid flapping of her wings builds up a *positive static electric charge*. "No way!" you think, but yes way, electrically charged bees are flying around everywhere all the time.

The pollen grains of a flower hold a negative charge, and when a bee lands in a flower, that fine pollen gets shaken loose from the flower's anther. It is attracted to the positively charged hairs on the bee's body, so it just leaps onto the bee without her even having to touch it.

By the way, there is a study showing some evidence that bees can actually sense the electric field of flowers with their hairs and, if a flower has lost too much of its negative charge, they know it has been depleted of pollen by other bees, and will avoid wasting effort and move on to a flower with a better energy field.

Mind blown? You're welcome.

After collecting all that pollen to her like a superhero with magnetic abilities, the bee uses her legs to wipe the pollen from her body either onto her abdomen or, depending on the species of bee, her hind legs. Admittedly, this is a much less impressive way to move pollen around, but who am I to criticize?

Once back in the nest, the forager cleans herself off and unloads her pollen haul into waiting pollen storage cells near the brood nest. It will be used to feed the young. And also those lazy-ass drones, at least until they're no longer needed for breeding.

Bees like the honeybee carry pollen on their hind legs, packed into "pollen baskets" which are really specialized leg hairs called corbiculae.

big ol' wads of pollen!

ALLOW ME TO WAX PHILOSOPHICAL

The Greek philosopher Aristotle thought that beeswax was a plant wax. He proposed that it was collected by bees from flowers and trees and then carried to the nest on their legs. Other Greek scholars of his time went on to make lists of what plants provided this wax, and even ranked the plants on which were best.

Later, in the mid-seventeenth century, some leading naturalists like the Dutch biologist Jan Swammerdam made a scientific leap forward and decided that wax was converted from pollen by the honeybees. These naturalists had conflicting ideas about exactly how it was done (e.g., was it pollen mixed with saliva, pollen mixed with honey, or maybe something in the stinger?), but they all agreed that wax came from pollen.

We now know that, in reality, beeswax is produced biologically by a worker bee—honey is metabolized into wax and secreted by wax glands in her abdomen. The tiny wafers of wax are collected by other workers who then use it to construct honeycomb cells.

Clearly, both the ancient Greek philosophers and those Renaissance jackwads had no real idea of what was actually going on inside a beehive at all. It kind of seems like they were just making shit up to sound smart.

Oh, by the way, a honeybee's wings beat about 200 times per second!

This is what makes that distinctive buzzing noise, and also what makes the hummingbird's average of about fifty-five beats per second seem pretty goddamn lazy by comparison.

Swarm in Here,
or Is It Just Me?

For most people, accidentally running across a bee swarm can be pretty freakin' alarming, because if you're just walking along minding your own business and you suddenly become aware of a great big writhing wad of bees, possibly dangling from a branch in your immediate vicinity, it can set off some fight-or-flight warning bells in you, and we all know who would win in this fight.

But tell your limbic system to calm down for a minute—in spite of what many people seem to believe, bees do not swarm because they are enraged and looking for revenge against humans for ruining the whole planet.

Swarming is how honeybee colonies divide and multiply, and it is a normal part of honeybee behavior. When a colony gets big enough, or if food sources are too scarce, the workers will stop feeding the queen for a while so that she stops laying eggs and loses weight. When she's slimmed down enough to make the flight, she leaves the hive and a portion of the colony follows her.

They find an initial resting spot close to the original hive where the swarm will congregate, like that branch above your head. Then a small group of scouts fly out in all directions in search of a good location for a new hive, returning to the swarm and using the waggle-dance to communicate what's available. Once they have decided on the best place, the swarm will leave this resting spot to form their new colony. Swarming bees can only carry as much honey as will fit in their stomachs, so they only have a brief time window to select a new nesting spot and get to it. They will usually move on within a few hours to their new home. If they don't, the new colony won't survive.

Because they have no brood to defend and they are preoccupied with finding a new nest for their queen, swarming bees are not typically aggressive, but they sure as hell will attack if they perceive

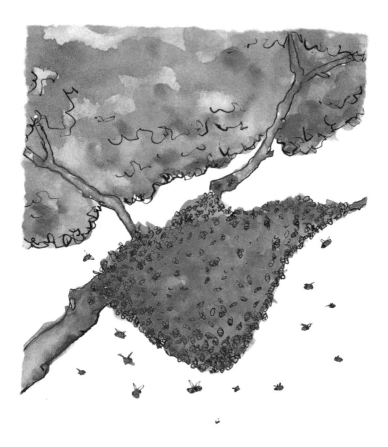

a threat to the colony. So keep your distance because, believe me, you don't want to be the dumbass who provokes them.

If a swarm is in a location that poses a danger, local beekeepers may be called in and can usually capture and safely remove a swarm to be relocated without harming the colony.

Meanwhile, the remaining workers in the original hive will either make a new queen or an existing virgin queen will be mated, but either way, someone is getting promoted and it's time to get on with everyday bee-business.

COOL BEES

Surprise, all bees are cool (obviously).
But I really want to impart to you just
how cool these *particular* bees are.

Fine, if you want to get pedantic, bees are technically kind of hot. They use their body heat and fan their wings to regulate the temperature inside the nest. The brood area must be kept at the optimum average temperature of 35 degrees Celsius year-round for the colony to survive. (That's 95 degrees Fahrenheit for those of us who live in a country that didn't have the common sense to metricate in the 1970s like the rest of the goddamn world.) Now can we please talk about these cool bees?

European Honeybee

Apis mellifera

Wow. I mean, what do you say about *Apis mellifera*?

When someone says the word "bee," odds are that you picture the European honeybee. *Apis mellifera* is probably THE most famous bee of all time, and they've earned it. They have been supplying humans with honey for thousands of years, and they still look fantastic. Their work as pollinators? Incredible. They make gathering pollen look easy. I think it's fair to say that we owe them a great debt, because modern agriculture worldwide would be totally screwed without honeybees. Credit where credit is due.

On top of that, these bees look so sharp with their perfect balance of aggressive lines, crisp black-and-yellow stripes, and just the right amount of soft fuzzy hairs to really pick up the pollen. They totally capture the essence of *bee-ness*, if you ask me.

I'm a huge fan of the European honeybee. I run into them all the time, and there are so many questions I'd like to ask, but I get starstruck. I always try to act nonchalant, but I end up grinning like a fool and blurting out something like "Honey is good!"

Oh my god, did I actually just yell "Honey is good"? They must think I'm a complete idiot.

(European Honeybee)

· makes honey!
· bee celeprity!
· so cool.

Apis mellifera

Yellow-Faced Bumblebee

Bombus vosnesenskii

I think we can all agree that these chonky little fuzzballs are freaking adorable. Just look at them. They are eusocial, like honeybees, with colonies of around two hundred that nest in dry hollows in the ground(!!). They are amazing at pollinating flowers and vegetables of many types, as if we even needed another reason to love them.

They're not terribly aggressive. They seem like pretty laid-back, go-with-the-flow type of bees—they're just living life, man. If you've ever seen them cruising around your garden in apparent slow motion, just happily bouncing from flower to flower in no particular hurry, then you know what I mean.

I bet they'd be so cool to hang with. You know, maybe have a beer or two and listen to a little reggae on the back deck while we trade tomato pollination stories.

Bombus vosnesenskii are native to the west coast of North America and can be found from British Columbia to Baja California, which is probably why they're so chill and relaxed.

yellowfaced
bumblebee

So fuzzy...

little wings for a big chon!

So chill...

omfg this chon-- is the best!!

Bombus vosnesenskii

World's Smallest Bee

Perdita minima

There might actually be smaller bees than this one, although who would ever know because, at around 2 mm [less than ⅛ inch] in length, you practically need a microscope just to see it. *Perdita minima* is a solitary mining bee found in the southwestern United States, where it makes its teeny-tiny solitary nest in the sandy soil.

Sadly, unless you are a bee scientist looking for them with your bee microscope, most likely you will never see one due to their minuscule nature. Also, they are sand colored, which does not help at all if you are looking for something in the desert.

Maybe because so few people normally see them, *Perdita minima* doesn't have a colloquial name other than "World's Smallest Bee," which is a shame because that sounds like an old carnival sideshow tent that didn't get many visitors. I think we can all agree that they deserve a catchier nickname—I would definitely call them "Li'l Beezies." Feel free to use that if you are a bee scientist.

The World's Smallest Bee!

Not this one

this one

yes, this is
drawn to scale.

(Uh, yes, it is.)

They're less than 2mm, so get off my back, ok.
What are you, the drawing police?

Perdita minima

Teddy Bear Bee

Amegilla bombiformis

Yes, I *did* say "Teddy Bear Bee." If you haven't been convinced yet that bees are cute, then this one should stop you in your tracks!

Its species name, *bombiformis*, means "form of a bumblebee." While this stout little bugger *could* be mistaken for a bumblebee, it is actually an Australian mason bee of the *Apidae* family, and it is covered in fuzzy, orange-brown fur like a teddy bear.

I am told that apparently a lot of people find teddy bears "lovable," god knows why, but personally I think teddy bears are creepy. Sure, they start out looking friendly, but after a while they get worn out and their fur gets dilapidated, and then they lose a little stuffing, and eventually they just have that one button eye hanging by a few frayed threads, but it's still looking at you . . . Ugh, no, thank you.

That said, I would agree that *A. bombiformis* is lovable and does, in fact, sort of look like a little bear-bee. Wait. Bears crossed with bees? Oh, hell yeah, I can definitely get behind that. Bear-bees all day long.

"teddy bear bee"

1. brownish
2. fuzzy
3. pleasantly plump

Amegilla bombiformis

Pantaloon Bee

Dasypoda hirtipes

Look at this bee!! The female has extremely hairy hind legs, which get just packed with pollen, making her look like she's wearing bright-yellow wide-leg pants! Technically this makes her the most fashion-forward of all the *Melittidae*.

D. hirtipes is also sometimes referred to as the "Hairy-Legged Mining Bee," which seems pretty unimaginative and, if you ask me, kind of mean-spirited. This is probably why someone with an eye for the sartorial, and enough empathy to understand that body-shaming is unacceptable, decided that *D. hirtipes* should be called the "Pantaloon Bee."

Also, wow, could someone please sew a very tiny black jacket and a pollen-yellow silk scarf for this bee??

pantaloon bee

fashionista legs!

damn!
look at all
that pollen...

pantaloon bees
can carry massive
amounts of pollen
because their hind
legs are so hairy.

(But be kind, no one
wants to be called a
"hairy legged mining bee.")

Dasypoda hirtipes

Squash Bee

Xenoglossa strenua

When people say "Squash Bee" they're really talking about one of two different yet related genera of the *Eucerini* tribe here, *Peponapis* and *Xenoglossa*. They're both called "Squash Bees." I know, but don't worry, though, because this particular ambiguity doesn't appear to bother the scientists or the bees for some reason.

In this case, we're looking at *Xenoglossa strenua*, a species of long-horned bee in the family *Apidae*, and, as the name would imply, the exciting news here is that these big beautiful bees are fantastic pollinators of squash! Yes, squash!

I know it's hard to get jazzed about squash, but just take a look at this big and fascinating bee.

They collect pollen from *Cucurbita* flowers, the females arriving in the morning, and the males showing up and staying later. The males sometimes find themselves trapped inside as the squash blossoms start to wilt over the course of the day, and they end up stuck in there overnight. We all know how embarrassing that is, am I right, fellas?

Squash bee

1. Pollinates the squash.
2. Males might get trapped in squash blossoms.
3. I mean, this could happen to anybody, really.

 squash is
ok, I guess.

Xenoglossa strenua

Heath Bumblebee

Bombus jonellus

Look at this little bumblebee!! The heath bumblebee is named for its preference for the flowers of the heathlands in Scotland and the Shetland Isles, but really they can be found in most of Europe, from Scandinavia to Spain, and even in large swaths of Asia, too.

Heath bumblebees are pretty small for bumblebees, the workers measuring only around 12 mm [about ½ inch], which is part of what makes them extra adorable. They're kind of like Shetland ponies, if Shetland ponies had white butts and could fly. Oh my god, winged, white-butted Shetland ponies buzzing around in your flower beds? Holy crap, that would be so cool! Although, now that I think of it, I guess flying ponies could potentially do a lot of damage to your garden. I'm torn on this one.

Heath bumblebee

White butt

likes:
- bog heather
- goldenrod
- various highland flowers

Bombus Jonellus

Chocolate Mining Bee

Andrena scotica

Sometimes called a "hawthorn bee," this honeybee-sized member of the family *Andrenidae* is a mining bee common to western Europe and frequently found throughout Great Britain. They are solitary, the females building their own nests and tending their own young, though interestingly they usually share a communal entrance to two or more (sometimes up to hundreds of) individual underground burrows.

Why are they referred to as "chocolate" mining bees? Well, possibly because they have a short, fine, brown-haired coat that makes them look like they might have been dusted in rich, dark cocoa powder. But before you go and get any dumb ideas, I'm just going to nip this in the bud and state, categorically, that chocolate mining bees do NOT taste like chocolate, and you should NOT try to eat one, even just to make sure for yourself.

Note: Other insects frequently parasitize *Andrena scotica* nests, including the cuckoo bee species *Nomada marshamella*, which, I hasten to add, does NOT taste like marshmallow.

Chocolate mining bee

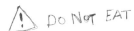 DO NOT EAT

FACT: does NOT taste like chocolate

Andrena scotica

Long-Horned Bee

Eucera longicornis

Holy shit, look at those horns!

We both know they're not really horns, but you get the idea. *E. longicornis* is a member of the *Apidae* tribe *Eucerini*, the long-horned bees. They are solitary ground-nesters, and they get their name from the male's ridiculously long antennae. Yeah, like as long as their head and body combined. I mean, obviously—what the hell else are you going to call them?

Eucerini occur all over the world. However, this handsome guy can be found in the Palearctic realm, which means mostly all of Eurasia and North Africa.

As with other long-horned bees, the females have much shorter horns. I mean, antennae.

Long-horned bee

Just look at those babies!

there's no real mystery why they've called "long-horned" bees, is there?

Eucera longicornis

Wallace's Giant Bee

Megachile pluto

This bee is one big mother! The female is larger than the male. With her whopping 2½ inch [6.4 cm] wingspan, a body the size of your whole damned thumb, and sporting some freaky-big mandibles, look out, because she is one impressive lady.

Not only is *Megachile pluto* the biggest damn bee known to us, but it was also thought to be extinct until 1981, and then not spotted again for almost forty years! The first picture and video footage of a live female was captured in Indonesia by an expedition in 2019.

Wallace's giant bee is actually a giant mason bee, but it was named after Alfred Russel Wallace,* who first collected it in 1858. Weirdly, Wallace himself didn't seem very interested in *M. pluto* and only jotted one line about it in his journal. WTF, Wallace? But whatever, a lot of other biologists are pretty obsessed with this huge, rare bee.

They are believed to be largely solitary, and they build their nests by drilling into an active colony of a particular tree-dwelling termite. Sneaky! The female uses her big, freaky mandibles to scrape tree resin into balls that are used to create reinforced compartments in her nest.

No one is 100 percent certain if they can really sting. A University of Sydney biologist who was a member of the 2019 expedition was quoted as saying, "We were all keen to get stung to see how bad it was, but because we only found the one we treated it very carefully."

Biologists, am I right?

* *Yes*, that *Alfred Russel Wallace, the one who also came up with the theory of evolution by natural selection at the same time as Charles Darwin, but didn't get famous like him. Tough break, Wallace.*

Wallace's Giant Bee

HOLY ~~SHIT~~
look at the size of this thing

badass
mandibles

4cm
long

body
the size
of your whole
thumb

regular honeybee size

6cm
wingspan

Megachile pluto

GREAT PAINTINGS, IF THEY HAD PUT BEES IN THEM

There have been a lot of great artists through the ages, but even they would admit that not every single one of their works turned out as well as some others.

I have noticed that in most of these "lesser" works, the artist seems to have omitted bees. Why? Who knows, but it obviously could have helped.

This made me think, "Wouldn't it be cool if I could go back in time and tell these artists about how awesome bees are, and then maybe they would have included a bee or two in their pieces, and who knows, it might have worked out pretty great!"

Sadly, time travel is beyond my ability. That is why I've included this section of some pretty good works of art, but showing how they could be improved with bees. I have included the comments I would share with the original artists.

I feel confident that if these artists were alive today, they would probably write a letter to thank me.

Boating

(1874)
ÉDOUARD MANET

Wow, let me just say, this has to be one of my favorite paintings of a gentleman in a white T-shirt. The straw-hat-and-mustache combo is a nice touch and would be considered very *en vogue* by many in my time. I'm not sure if it would be considered ironic or not, as the distinction was largely lost in the early twenty-first century due to hipsters getting out of hand.

Anyway, I have always felt that your paintings capture the leisure class being bored so well. Just look at this lady in the boat—she definitely has no effs to give!

But let me get to the point: Have you considered adding a bumblebee to this painting? That would really dial it up!

That straw-hat dude already looks low-key irritated, like, "The hell is that damned bee doing in the middle of this lake?" And she's all, "Chill, James, at least that bee has a purpose in life." Just think about it.

The Dance Class

(1874)
EDGAR DEGAS

Mr. Degas, I am a big, big fan of your paintings, so don't get me wrong; this is a pretty good one. Great color palette and stuff! Seriously, love the dancers! But the scene is a little dull, don't you think? It's like everyone is just standing around *before* anything is happening. I think a few bees in the studio would really spice things up!

You're welcome!

Madonna and Child

(CA. 1290–1300)
DUCCIO DI BUONINSEGNA

I couldn't help noticing your painting of the Madonna and Child.

I must say, the way you rendered the folds and volume of the drapery of the clothing is quite impressive, at least for the early fourteenth century. Nice work.

But, please forgive me for saying this, your Virgin looks a bit sad. Perhaps you intended this to show that she is aware of her child's inevitable crucifixion? Masterful, but depressing.

Also, your Christ Child looks more like a tiny middle-aged man than a real baby.

Frankly, these problems are common to most icon paintings of your time and will be repeated, much like this image, over and over for hundreds of years with very little innovation.

But don't worry—*this is a great opportunity for you to really stand out!* Imagine what the addition of a bee or two could do to liven up this dreary scene!

You will get noticed in a way that your contemporaries wouldn't even dream of!

Venus with Cupid the Honey Thief

(CA. 1580–1620)
COPY AFTER LUCAS CRANACH THE ELDER

Man, how refreshing it was to see your painting of Venus and Cupid! Really. A lot of German Renaissance painters would have completely phoned this type of thing in, but you put a bunch of bees in the starring role! Way ahead of your time, my friend.

Can I just say that casting Cupid as a honey thief was effing genius. Everyone hates that little butthole. I'm sure there's some kind of clever symbolism about sex and love here, and that's important subtext for the art-history nerds. But what makes this painting a total winner is that the audience gets what it wants, and that is to see the bees finally give that honeycomb-grabbing little cherub exactly what he has coming to him: payback!

Love how Cupid looks up to Venus, as if for sympathy, but she's gazing at us in an aside, telling the viewer what we all really want to say: "That's what you get when you steal from bees, stupid!"

Also, that hat you put on Venus? Incredible.

I almost hate to bring it up, but if I could offer just one tiny note for you: maybe just a few more bees? Not too many, but maybe fifteen to twenty? You know, really make it a slam-bang ending!

Other than that, perfection!

DVM PVER ALVEOLO FVRATVR MELLA CVPIDO,
FVRANTI DIGITVM SEDVLA PVNXIT APIS.
SIC ETIAM NOBIS BREVIS ET MORITVRA VOLVPTAS.
QVAM PETIMVS TRISTI MIXTA DOLORE NOCET.

SERIOUS
BEE
STUFF

It's all fun and games until someone dies out as a species. Bees, not to mention a whole lot of insects, appear to be headed in that direction, and trust me, this should set off some warning bells, because if the bees die off, it is some seriously bad news for the rest of us.

Agricultural practices, global warming, and disease are just some of the reasons that bee numbers are in decline on a global scale, and experts are legitimately freaked about this because it has an impact on world food supplies.

We live in a pretty delicately balanced system, and as hard as it can be to wrap your head around the enormous complexity of it, you can rest assured that everything is interconnected.

This means if you throw one little thing out of whack, there is a ripple effect that can have huge consequences, even ones we can't anticipate. For example, one seemingly insignificant flower stops growing, and suddenly a certain bug that only nests in that flower's leaves disappears, and then the bird that relies on that bug to feed its young—well, you get the idea. It's a house of cards, and if it collapses it will be a real shitshow for us as a species.

Bees are especially important when it comes to keeping our ecosystem working, and therefore are super important to our continued existence as a species. If bees were to go extinct, we'd be in big, big trouble. Rather than writing a whole dissertation on it, I'm going to boil it down into a few of the more critical points.

Pollination

Bees play a critical role in pollination. Of all the animals, bees are the most dominant pollinators of wild and crop plants. In fact, if you look at the evolutionary spread of flowering plants, it pretty much coincides with the evolutionary spread of bees.

Bees visit over 90 percent of the world's top 107 crops and are crucial for the growth of a huge number of plants, including those that we rely on for food. Some scientists believe that if bees were to die out, we would no longer be able to sustain crops like apples, coffee, cocoa, tomatoes, and almonds, among many others. Good luck trying to live without apple pie, coffee, chocolate, pizza, and almond milk.

SCIENTISTS SAY THAT BEES POLLINATE ONE IN THREE MOUTHFULS WE EAT!

I know!! This sounds super gross and it sort of ruined my lunch when I read it, but don't worry—it turns out this just means that about a third of all the crops we grow depend directly on pollination by bees. Scientists, why would you not just say it that way in the first place?

Animals and Livestock

Herbivores that depend on certain plants pollinated by bees will have a hard time surviving if bees go extinct. Cattle, which we rely on for meat and milk, are dependent on a diet of alfalfa, and hogs on a diet of feed corn (both of which are pollinated mostly by, you guessed it, bees). That would put a pretty big dent in the typical US diet.

Other herbivores like deer and rabbits would also likely have a hard time surviving and would begin to die off as their food sources disappeared. Carrion eaters like vultures and coyotes would probably make out pretty well, at least in the beginning.

Fuel

Canola, which most of us know as a cooking oil, relies on pollination by bees. It is also used extensively to produce biofuel. If we lost this source of biofuel it might put additional pressure on us to rely on fossil fuels.

Cotton

Cotton is dependent on pollination, so if bees disappeared, it would lead to a massive reduction in cotton production. The last time I looked, a lot of our most comfortable clothes are made from cotton. Hope you enjoy wearing polyester pants as you starve in our hellish post-bee apocalypse world.

The Land

Because a lot of plants will be unable to grow, grasslands will slowly become barren. Further into the future, large-scale desertification of once-fertile land will occur around the planet. Without plants to control erosion, landslides will wipe out whole towns, and winds will create massive dust storms. Ultimately, Earth will become one big desert littered with polyester-clad skeletons.

Admittedly, these scenarios are a matter of conjecture. How things would truly play out in the aftermath of a mass bee extinction is not certain. Experts disagree on exactly how important bees are and what precisely would happen. That is a problem with experts: They are always disagreeing on everything. But the majority of experts who don't have their heads up their own asses do agree that, if bees disappear, it's a bad, bad thing for all of us.

Do you like apples ←?

↑ because Bees are pollinating them for you.

GIVE BEES A CHANCE

Shit, it's pretty dire, right? If the bees go, the whole show ends and so do we. But there are some things that you and I can reasonably do to give bees a break and help them survive. And we sort of owe it to them, don't we?

Plant a Bee Garden

One of the biggest threats to bees is the continuing loss of habitat where they can forage for food and obtain a variety of nutrients that they need for colony survival. One of the best things you can do is create a habitat corridor full of plants rich in pollen and nectar. You don't need to have a lot of space, either. In fact, you don't even need to have a yard, because bees don't care if you have a garden, window boxes, or pots on your fire escape.

Choose bee-friendly plants (see page 108). Preferably choose ones that are native to the area you live in, and, if you can, plant patches of them, or at least multiples of each kind close to each other. Bees generally only visit one type of plant per trip, and you should try to make it worth their time. Putting in plants that flower at different times is a real bonus because it helps the bees have an ongoing source of food through the season.

Go Natural

Haha, no, you can get those highlights if you want to. By "go natural," I mean that you should forget about using pesticides, herbicides, and chemical fertilizers in your lawn and garden. They really mess with bees—and most other pollinator insects, for that matter. Real talk: It's time to switch to natural and organic gardening products.

Bee-Friendly Flowers

Cosmos
Mint
Asters
Lavender
Rosemary
Snapdragons
Cornflowers
Sunflowers
Bluebells
Thyme
Sedums
Calendulas
Clover
Zinnias
Phlox

Clematis
Digitalis
Crocus
Echinacea
Poppies
Strawberries
Sage
Fennel
Cilantro
Hollyhocks
Buttercup
Catnip
Dahlia
Honeysuckle
Summer Squash

Marigold
Geraniums
Butterfly Weed
Hyacinth
Blueberries
Hostas
Goldenrod
Bee Balm
Chives
Lupine
Nasturtium
Peony
Pansy

Let It Grow

A lot of you are not going to like hearing this, but it would really help if we stopped our never-ending and unwinnable war on weeds. Like it or not, dandelions, clover, and other flowering weeds are a vital food source to bees, not to mention food and habitat for a variety of other insect species as well. So let those weeds do their thing. If that's a nonstarter in your family, at least try to hold off on the weeding until the bees have had a chance to forage the blooms. A perfect lawn is a pretty bleak sight for a bee.

Rethink Your Perfect Lawn

We really should try to see weeds as the beneficial wild plants that they are and leave them alone, but let's be realistic—in many neighborhoods, there is a special kind of shame attached to having a front lawn full of dandelions. Because I guess for some reason we thought we needed yet another arbitrary and unrealistic societal expectation that helps us disapprove of ourselves and others.

It's deeply ingrained in American culture, but perhaps once we have learned to accept our own bodies and live our own truths or whatever, we could also let go of this dandelion thing. In the meantime, the obvious solution is to get rid of your whole dumb lawn.

I mean, COME ON, really. A big field of grass that you have to pour water and fertilizer on in order to keep it green? When it grows (and, in case you weren't aware, that is sure as shit exactly what grass does when you water and fertilize it), you are required to spend all day ruining the peace and quiet of the whole neighborhood by using an eighty-pound fume-spewing, gasoline-burning engine with blades, just to chop it all down and make it look like a carpet instead of grass, which is what your lawn is actually made out of.

Look me in the eyes and tell me that doesn't sound stupid.

"But what can I do?" you ask. Simple. Rip that water-wasting, time-sucking, suburban ego-carpet right the hell out of the ground and put in something better, like a rain garden with bee-friendly native plants and bushes. Or turn the whole thing into a flowering meadow with native grasses and wildflowers. No more mowing. No more weeding. Looks great. Saves the bees. Time for lemonade. You're welcome.

Bonus! Tell everyone about how you sacrificed your grass to save the bees and the planet—now you can feel great about yourself and give your lawn-shaming neighbors the finger while they feel bad about having perfectly manicured, dandelion-free yards. Total reversal, assholes!

Plant a Tree

Actually, plant as many as you can, because bees get a lot of their nectar and pollen from trees when they flower. Additionally, trees provide important habitats as well as nesting material for bees that use resin or tree leaves. Also, uh, birds and clean air? Trees are an incredibly important part of our ecology and climate. Duh.

Make a Home for Bees

Outside of honeybees, the majority of bees live underground, in holes in trees, or in hollow stems. You can help out the bumblebees just by leaving some areas of ground untouched so they have a safe place to make their nest. You can also buy or build "bee condos," which are made up of small tubes that bees can move into.

Build a Bee Bath

Yep, believe it or not, bees need water too. A shallow birdbath or even a bowl filled with clean water can really help a thirsty bee out. Put a few rocks or something in there so that they break the surface and give the bees a place to land for a drink.

Support Your Local Beekeeper

Beekeepers work hard to protect and nurture bees, and they often produce a variety of bee-related products in addition to honey, like candles and soaps. Buy some from your local beekeeper. This one is pretty easy.

In Case of Bumblebee Emergency

If you find a bumblebee that looks like it is struggling and can't fly, it's probably resting. This is normal, so leave it the hell alone. But if it has been grounded for more than forty-five minutes, that could mean it is in trouble and it might need your help. The best thing to do is to just gently place the bumblebee into a bee-friendly flower. Done and done.

Wait, what if you don't have any bee-friendly flowers handy? Oh my god, what even are the bee-friendly flowers again? I knew I should have made a list of bee-friendly flowers and kept it in my wallet and OH MY GOD THIS BEE NEEDS HELP WHAT DO I DO?!

For starters, try to calm down a bit. Then make a fifty-fifty mix of white sugar and water, put a little bit into a spoon or a bottle cap, and then offer it politely to the bumblebee. Try to give the mixture to the front end of the bee—if this part is confusing to you, you might want to get someone else to handle this operation. Ideally, do this in a sheltered place where the little bee won't get stepped on. The sugar water can give the bee the energy it needs to get off the ground and back into bumblebee action.

IMPORTANT NOTE! Please remember, this is a onetime, emergency sort of deal! Sugar water messes with their dietary needs, so don't be just slinging it around willy-nilly, no matter how badly you want to be popular with bees.

1:1 Sugar-Water Mix

- Use white sugar, baby.
- Never use honey, honey.
  (it might have pathogens 💀 for bees)

from CM

- whisper words of encouragement.

One Last Thing

I know, it feels hard. All of this is a lot of change to how we do things. But just think about this: no bees, no plants and trees, no birds. And then what is your cat going to eat?

Like it or not, our yards and gardens are part of the ecosystem; our decisions as individuals and communities have impacts on our climate and environment. What we do affects bees, and we'd better start acting like it before we're all screwed.

ACKNOWLEDGMENTS

Making a book is a team effort, and I want to sincerely thank everyone at Chronicle Books who helped make this one possible. Special thanks to my editor, Becca, for her partnership, skill, and sense of humor, and for just being great to work with.

Many thanks to my agent, Rosie, for her ongoing support and for always being in my corner. That, and being ready to rock and roll whenever I need something, be it professional advice, a sounding board, or just a good pep talk.

My family has always grounded me in love and laughter. I owe them a great deal, especially my wife, whose unwavering support, patience, and occasional raised eyebrow keep me going in more ways than she knows.

Finally, I want to acknowledge my readers. I am still sometimes surprised that you like my books so much, but it feels great to be valued, so thank you for your enthusiasm and support. You make it possible for me to keep doing what I love, which is putting new and sometimes weird things into the world for others to enjoy. I am truly grateful for the opportunity.

REFERENCES

Abramson, Charles I., et al. "Operant Conditioning in Honey Bees (*Apis mellifera* L.): The Cap Pushing Response." *PLOS ONE* 11, no. 9 (2016): e0162347. https://doi.org/10.1371/journal.pone.0162347.

Barron, Andrew. "The Honey Bee Brain." Templeton World Charity Foundation. YouTube Video, July 12, 2019. https://www.youtube.com/watch?v=N_wei1OdK0E.

BBC. *Behind the Beehive: The Code.* Episode 2. YouTube Video, July 27, 2011. https://www.youtube.com/watch?v=F5rWmGe0HBI.

Briggs, Helen. "Prehistoric Farmers Were First Beekeepers." *BBC News*, November 11, 2015. https://www.bbc.com/news/science-environment-34749846.

Brunet, Johanne. "Pollinator Decline: Implications for Food Security & Environment." *Scientia*, June 26, 2019. https://www.scientia.global/pollinator-decline-implications-for-food-security-environment.

Buchman, Steve. "*Perdita minima*—'World's Smallest Bee.'" U.S. Forest Service. https://www.fs.fed.us/wildflowers/pollinators/pollinator-of-the-month/perdita_minima.shtml.

C., Hannah. "How Do Bees Drink Nectar Exactly?" *Science Times*, August 11, 2020. https://www.sciencetimes.com/articles/26838/20200811/bees-drink-nectar-exactly.htm.

Davis, Nicola. "Goal! Bees Can Learn Ball Skills from Watching Each Other, Study Finds." *The Guardian*, February 23, 2017. https://www.theguardian.com/science/2017/feb/23/goal-bees-can-learn-ball-skills-from-watching-each-other-study-finds.

Donkersley, Philip. "Bees: How Important Are They and What Would Happen If They Went Extinct?" *The Conversation*, August 19, 2019. http://the conversation.com/bees-how-important-are-they-and-what-would-happen-if-they-went-extinct-121272.

Dunning, Hayley. "Bee Brains as You Have Never Seen Them Before." Imperial College London News, February 24, 2016. https://www.imperial .ac.uk/news/171050/bee-brains-have-never-seen-them.

Embry, Paige. *Our Native Bees: America's Endangered Pollinators and the Fight to Save Them.* Portland, OR: Timber Press, 2018.

Engel, Michael S. "Notes on the Classification of *Ctenocolletes* (Hymenoptera: Stenotritidae)." *Journal of Melittology* 92 (2019): 1–6. https://doi .org/10.17161/jom.v0i92.12073.

Hanson, Thor. *Buzz: The Nature and Necessity of Bees.* New York: Basic Books, 2018.

Hepburn, H. R. *Honeybees and Wax: An Experimental Natural History.* Berlin: Springer-Verlag, 1986.

Jarimi, Hasila, et al. "A Review on Thermoregulation Techniques in Honey Bees' (*Apis mellifera*) Beehive Microclimate and Its Similarities to the Heating and Cooling Management in Buildings." *Future Cities and Environment* 6, no. 1 (2020): 7. https://doi.org/10.5334/fce.81.

Karihaloo, B. L., et al. "Honeybee Combs: How the Circular Cells Transform into Rounded Hexagons." *Journal of the Royal Society Interface* 10, no. 86 (2013): 20130299. https://doi.org/10.1098/rsif.2013.0299.

Krulwich, Robert. "What Is It About Bees and Hexagons?" *Krulwich Wonders*, NPR, May 14, 2013. https://www.npr.org/sections/ krulwich/2013/05/13/183704091/what-is-it-about-bees-and-hexagons.

Loukola, Olli J., et al. "Bumblebees Show Cognitive Flexibility by Improving on an Observed Complex Behavior." *Science* 355, no. 6327 (2017): 833–36. https://doi.org/10.1126/science.aag2360.

Mayo Clinic Staff. "Honey." Mayo Clinic, November 14, 2020. https://www.mayoclinic.org/drugs-supplements-honey/art-20363819.

Michener, Charles D. *The Bees of the World.* Baltimore: Johns Hopkins University Press, 2000.

Millar, Helen. "The Importance of Bees to Humans, the Planet, and Food Supplies." *Medical News Today*, May 18, 2021. https://www.medicalnewstoday.com/articles/why-are-bees-important-to-humans.

Patel, Vidushi, et al. "Why Bees Are Critical for Achieving Sustainable Development." *Ambio* 50, no. 1 (2021): 49–59. https://doi.org/10.1007/s13280-020-01333-9.

Petruzzello, Melissa. "What Would Happen If All the Bees Died?" *Encyclopedia Britannica*. https://www.britannica.com/story/what-would-happen-if-all-the-bees-died.

Quenqua, Douglas. "The World's Largest Bee Is Not Extinct." *The New York Times*, February 21, 2019. https://www.nytimes.com/2019/02/21/science/giant-bee-wallace.html.

Tarpy, David. "The Honey Bee Dance Language." *NC State Extension Publications*. February 23, 2016. https://content.ces.ncsu.edu/honey-bee-dance-language.

Vickers, Hannah. "Why Are Bees Important? And How You Can Help Them." Woodland Trust, July 17, 2018. https://www.woodlandtrust.org.uk/blog/2018/07/why-are-bees-important-and-how-you-can-help-them.

Zakon, Harold H. "Electric Fields of Flowers Stimulate the Sensory Hairs of Bumble Bees." *Proceedings of the National Academy of Sciences* 113, no. 26 (2016): 7020. https://doi.org/10.1073/pnas.1607426113.

Zhang, Shaowu, et al. "Honeybee Memory: A Honeybee Knows What to Do and When." *Journal of Experimental Biology* 209, no. 22 (2006): 4420–28. https://doi.org/10.1242/jeb.02522.

PHOTO CREDITS

The Metropolitan Museum of Art, New York, Buoninsegna, Duccio di. *Madonna and Child.* https://www.metmuseum.org/art/collection/search/438754.

The Metropolitan Museum of Art, New York, Degas, Edgar. *The Dance Class.* https://www.metmuseum.org/art/collection/search/438817.

The Metropolitan Museum of Art, New York, Manet, Édouard. *Boating.* https://www.metmuseum.org/art/collection/search/436947.

The Metropolitan Museum of Art, New York, *Venus with Cupid the Honey Thief.* Robert Lehman Collection. https://www.metmuseum.org/art/collection/search/459077.

GENERAL REFERENCE WEBSITES

American Bee Journal. https://americanbeejournal.com.
The Bee Conservancy. https://thebeeconservancy.org.
Bumblebee Conservation Trust. https://www.bumblebeeconservation.org.
BuzzAboutBees.Net. https://www.buzzaboutbees.net.
Entomological Society of America. https://entsoc.org.
Honey Bee Suite. https://www.honeybeesuite.com.
iNaturalist. https://www.inaturalist.org.
PNW Bumble Bee Atlas. https://www.pnwbumblebeeatlas.org.
Puget Sound Beekeepers Association. https://www.pugetsoundbees.org.
Wikipedia. https://www.wikipedia.org.
World Wildlife Fund. https://www.worldwildlife.org.

Seventeen Bees I'd Like to Hang Out With

1. *Halictus tripartitus*
2. *Apis nigrocincta*
3. *Agapostemon angelicus*
4. *Andrena scotica*
5. *Bombus ternarius*
6. *Melissodes robustior*
7. *Andrena prunorum*
8. *Syntrichalonia exquisita*
9. *Peponapis pruinosa*
10. *Andrena auricoma*
11. *Bombus hypnorum*
12. *Nomada ochrohirta*
13. *Bombus perplexus*
14. *Apis dorsata*
15. *Apis florea*
16. *Xylocopa tabaniformis*
17. *Bombus insularis*

SOME GOOD Bee CONVERSATION STARTERS:

→ So, what's it like to be a sweat bee?

→ LOVE your look!
(compliment her amazing orange belt)

→ Let's ~~talk~~ talk favorite squashes...

→ You seem so chill. What's your secret?

→ You had me at "giant honeybee".
(a little flirty)

→ "Indiscriminate cuckoo bumblebee"?
Okay, spill...

FAVORITE BEES IN MY GARDEN RIGHT NOW

1. HAZEL — sweet, easy going, forgiving

2. MAUDIA — never says a bad word about anybody

3. LOIS — serious and fun (but not at the same time)

4. BERTHA — kind, devoted

5. HELEN — secretly mischievous

6. VONNIE — makes friends easily, does things her own way

7. PATSY — loud and fun

List Your Favorite Things about Bees

1. _____
2. _____
3. _____
4. _____
5. _____
6. _____
7. _____
8. _____
9. _____
10. _____
11. _____
12. _____
13. _____
14. _____
15. _____
16. _____
17. _____
18. _____
19. _____
20. _____
21. _____
22. _____
23. _____
24. _____
25. _____
26. _____

27. _____
28. _____
29. _____
30. _____
31. _____
32. _____
33. _____
34. _____
35. _____
36. _____
37. _____
38. _____
39. _____
40. _____
41. _____
42. _____
43. _____
44. _____
45. _____
46. _____
47. _____
48. _____
49. _____
50. _____
51. _____
52. _____
53. _____
54. _____
55. _____
56. _____
57. _____
58. _____

59. _____

60. _____

61. _____

62. _____

63. _____

64. _____

65. _____

66. _____

67. _____

68. _____

69. _____

70. _____

71. _____

72. _____

73. _____

74. _____

75. _____

76. _____

77. _____

78. _____

79. _____

80. _____

81. _____

82. _____

83. _____

84. _____

85. _____

86. _____

87. _____

This should at least get you started listing what is great about bees. You can staple some extra sheets of paper to this one when you need to add more.